Mentoring Like Barnabas

Mentoring Like Barnabas

Mitsuo Fukuda

Translated by
Simon Cozens

Wide Margin

Published in 2011 by Wide Margin,

90 Sandyleaze, Gloucester, GL2 0PX, UK

http://www.wide-margin.co.uk/

Initially published as
"BARUNABA NO YOU NI HITO WO SODATERU"
(バルナバのように人を育てる)
by World of Life Press (いのちのことば社)

ISBN 978-0-9565943-9-6

Printed and bound in Great Britain by
Lightning Source, Milton Keynes

Contents

Translator's Foreword

Mentoring is a key process for personal development, and this book will show you how to become a mentor to those that God has placed around you. It will introduce you to techniques and skills for mentoring, of course, but more importantly it will show you the attitude of heart and mind required to handle the task with reverence, confidence and love. Above all it will remind you that the task of mentoring and personal development belongs to God, and it can show you how to help and be a part in what God is already doing in people's lives.

Coming out of the Japanese social and church context, it contains much which is of huge benefit to those working in Japan, but its message is much wider than that: that the whole Church throughout the world can and should become a society where people see the potential and the abilities of others and help them to move into the work that God has prepared for them. But one of the particular benefits of its Japanese background is that it is aimed towards church members who often lack confidence in their abilities and feel that 'church work' is more appropriately done by 'church professionals.' One of Dr. Fukuda's aims in his teaching is to demonstrate how God's work is something that each and every believer can join in.

Mitsuo Fukuda is well-known in the Japanese church as a leader in the house church movement, a writer on issues of contextualization and leadership, and a mentor and coach to a generation of emerging leaders. He is particularly skilled in distilling complex and seemingly intimidating ideas and presenting them with clarity and simplicity; his writing, as a reflection of the very mentoring style he teaches here, inspires confidence and urges his readers to trust themselves to God's leading and watch with wonder at what He can do through them, things that they may have previously thought impossible.

This has certainly been my experience on reading and contemplating this book; it has been a great blessing to me, and my hope and my prayer is that it will become the same to you.

Foreword to the original edition

Mentoring Like Barnabas stands to be a ground-breaking work in the field of leadership and ministry development. I know firsthand how influential coaching can be: I've seen lives, churches, and ministries transformed by its power. I have no doubt that through Dr. Fukuda's excellent book, countless Japanese ministries will benefit as well.

When coaching was first introduced in Japan in the late 1980's, it was a totally new concept. Yet it's one that is absolutely crucial for effective ministry in Japan today. The Barnabas role of coming alongside to help others as they discover their God-given vision is of critical importance as Christian leaders strive to raise up a new generation of leaders and help churches attain increasing health and vitality.

The need for people to come alongside others to empower them is particularly great in societies that are more vertically oriented. The movement from authority-based **instruction** to supportive **partnership** represents a significant step forward for developing more effective leadership structures. Barnabas-style ministry holds the key to raising up strong, confident new leaders, especially in the Japanese context. In this book, Dr. Fukuda masterfully adapts coaching concepts, contextualizing them into the Japanese situation.

I am delighted that Dr. Fukuda has written this very important book that helps unpack the concept of Barnabas ministries for Japan. I strongly encourage you to read, ponder, and put into practice the valuable material Dr. Fukuda has set forth in these pages. May the Lord bless you as you read and may he powerfully use Barnabas ministries to bring in a greater harvest for the advance of God's kingdom.

Dr. Robert E. Logan,
CoachNet International Ministries

Barnabas-style leadership

Hoshi Ittetsu's way of thinking

In the sixties in Japan, comics about sport were incredibly popular, and many of them were made into cartoons and shown on TV.

One of the most famous was called "The Star of the Giants". It was the story of a young boy called Hoshi Hyuuma, who dreams of becoming a baseball player for the Tokyo Yomiuri Giants, one of Japan's major league baseball teams, and it tells of how he finally joins the team and plays as a pitcher.

The antagonist in this story is Hyuuma's father, Hoshi Ittetsu. He used to be a famous player for the Giants, one of the best in the team's history, but for some reason left the team, and after that, became totally consumed by the idea of bringing up his son Hyuuma to be a first-class player.

I think Hoshi Ittetsu trained Hyuuma in three characteristic ways:

First, there was the force of his vision. His favourite phrase was "Be a shining star in the constellation of the Giant!" He certainly had a vision that he laid out before his son, and his vision was a great success in motivating Hyuuma.

But the vision that he had did not put his son's happiness first—it was a vision driven by Ittetsu's own dreams and values. Fundamentally, he used his son as a tool to deal with the failures and regrets of his past. Perhaps you could say he sent his son out to fight a proxy war against the world on his behalf.

Second, the mentoring relationship that Ittetsu had with his son involved a lot of scolding and motivation through harsh words. Ittetsu always made his young son wear "Major League Bowl Training Casts" to develop his muscles, and he often demanded that Hyuuma "go for it" to the very limits of his physical strength. He closed his ears to his son's feelings, and hardly ever gave you the impression that he was the sort of person who would play with his son, hug him, or praise him. His idea of motivation would be to give him a loud pep talk. He was rigid, he was uncompromising, and he was forceful in his vision—but it looked like he thought that was the only way to achieve his dream.

Third, he focused exclusively on achieving a goal. Even Hyuuma himself, in the second half of the story, describes himself as a "baseball robot", and he complains to his friends that he was brought up believing that baseball was everything in his life. For him, achieving the goal of being a first class baseball player for the

Giants was his all-consuming purpose. And when you look at the relationships he had with other people in his life, you can see what that did to him: Ittetsu may have developed Hyuuma's muscles, but his character and personality was totally undeveloped.

How much of an Ittetsu are you?

I've given a long description of "Star of the Giants", but that's because I think it can teach us a lot. I'd like you to look down the following checklist and see if any of these factors apply to you–let's calculate your degree of "Hoshi Ittetsu-ness".

• When someone comes to you for advice, you sometimes catch yourself jumping in with stories of your own before you've really finished listening to what they were saying.

• You sometimes talk with your friends about how the doctrines that you have learned or the traditions of the church group that you belong to are better than others'. Alternatively, you might not need to say it, because the way you talk makes people realise that you take it as read.

• The words "should" and "must" appear in your sentences rather more than they do in other people's.

• At least once in the last week, you weren't able to take the time that you wanted to talk at leisure to a family member or loved one.

- Phrases like "Go for it!" or "Hang in there!" come out of your mouth.

- If you were to be honest, at the bottom of your heart, there's a feeling that says, "if I'm not the best in everything that I do, I won't be satisfied."

- You've been accused of being rather pushy.

- You wouldn't say it out loud, but there have been times that you've thought in your heart, "if something's not working out, you should just give up on it."

- You're usually busy, but you're not often taking the time out for your own personal development.

Hoshi Ittetsu's style of leadership is quite closely connected with the cultural worldview of the Japanese, so I think many people in Japan will be able to associate with the above questions. However, busyness, pushiness and dogmatic certainty are not just found in Japan—any of us can be like this, and carry it over into the way we coach and mentor others. But I want to show that this way of raising up people is unscriptural in at least three areas.

First, because someone who leads like this is concerned primarily with pushing forth their own vision, God's vision can get lost or obstructed.

Second, it is difficult for their followers to develop and maintain a healthy self-image, as this style of leadership restricts the self-determination of their followers.

Third, this kind of leadership tends to concentrate on achievement and getting things done–to the detriment of human relationships.

The leader as seen in Ephesians

This is how church leaders are portrayed in the Bible:

> It was he who gave some as apostles, some as prophets, some as evangelists, and some as pastors and teachers, to equip the saints for the work of ministry, that is, to build up the body of Christ, until we all attain to the unity of the faith and of the knowledge of the Son of God–a mature person, attaining to the measure of Christ's full stature. (Ephesians 4:11-13)

What this is saying is that the role of the leader is to be a catalyst; their job is to draw out the latent potential that God has given to His people, and to give people what they need for the work of ministry that God has given to them. The Bible says that if we help people to do this, their growth will continue until they become spiritual adults and they can achieve the calling that God has placed upon their lives.

This kind of nurturing work is not just given exclusively to those who have the title of "'teacher" or "pastor" or "vicar"–actually it's a job that's been given to every single believer. Why? Because there is a cycle of personal development in the church. Those who have been discipled must continue to develop until they can disciple and train others, or the cycle will be broken–and if that cycle is broken, then only the only people actively participating in ministry will be those who have been given official qualifications and positions: everybody else will become passive, becoming merely the "recipients" of ministry.

So both leaders and followers need to be aiming for the same thing–both sets of people need to be in the process of maturing themselves until they can mentor others. Think about how this will transform the church! Those who see themselves as teachers now will start to see their ministry as preparing others; those who see themselves as adminstrators now will start to see their ministry as encouraging others; those who work towards fulfilling their own dreams and visions now will start to work towards helping their neighbours realize their dreams and visions.

This kind of leadership–mentoring and developing others–is like the catalyst in a chemical reaction, or the pacemaker who sets the pace for marathon runners.

Barnabas-style leadership

You can find a great example of this style of mentoring-based leadership in the Bible. It's the style of a man from Cyprus called Joseph.

According to Acts 4:36, they gave him the nickname "Barnabas". It means the "son of consolation." What a great name to be given. It means "the one who draws alongside others to help them." Barnabas drew alongside people to help them to achieve the call that God had put upon their lives. Steven Ogne and Tom Nebel identify four ways in which Barnabas raised up and guided people:

First, he saw the call on Paul's life, and the latent potential that he had, even though Paul had formerly persecuted the church. Barnabas brought him to the disciples–which allowed Paul to find his place in ministry. (Acts 9:27)

Second, he was sent out together with Paul and he worked in partnership with him, experiencing both harvest and persecution together. (Acts 13)

Third, he opposed Paul when it came to John Mark, because Barnabas saw the need to support John Mark's personal development even at a possible cost to the mission. (Acts 15:39)

Fourth, he rejoiced when those he had mentored ended up surpassing him. In Acts 11:30, the Bible talks about "Barnabas and Paul"–Barnabas' name is first. But by 13:50, Luke is writing about "Paul and Barnabas".

Can we become mentors like Barnabas? I'm sure some readers might think that if only they themselves had been mentored by someone like Barnabas, then they'd be able to mentor others the way Barnabas did. That's certainly true in one way, but don't forget that God is good. He has the best possible plan for you. He thinks of you as His beloved child, and so will not fail to work with you to develop your character. Barnabas himself had an excellent mentor: Barnabas was mentored by God.

Support and Challenge

*The most important thing
is... they have to want it.*

"Follow Me": A play in one act

Watanabe hurried along the road to the training hall. Along the way, he met a couple of students walking along with something of a serious look on their faces. Looking a little closer, they were juniors from the judo club of Watanabe's old high school.

"Hey you guys, why the long faces? Hold your heads up when you walk!"

"Oh, sorry, Watanabe-sempai. Since you used to be in the judo club, don't you know what's happening today? Today is the first day of trials for the national championships."

"It's not the finals today, how am I supposed to remember all the details like that? Anyway, if it's only the first day, there can't be any major problems, right?"

"Well, sure, we won, but Tanaka broke a bone in the main event."

"You mean Tanaka who won the individual prize last year?"

"Yeah, and this year he thought he might have a shot at the nationals... But now there's no way Tanaka can play in a match. We'd really worked hard until today, but now I just can't help thinking that all that work was for nothing."

"Guys, buck up and stop whining. You've still got Yamada and Suzuki, right? What good is being so worried going to do you? If you've got time to whinge, then you've got time to practice. Right, I'm going to see if I've still got it in me. Shut up and follow me!"

Dealing with others at your own pace

Let's think about how Watanabe dealt with his juniors:

First, even though the juniors had come up against an unexpected accident which threw them into a panic, he did not want to understand their feelings. He didn't stop to notice their frustration and uncertainty and anger, but instead excused himself by saying that he couldn't be expected to remember the opening day of the competition.

Even after the juniors had expressed their problems, he offended them even further with insensitive words. For instance, pep talks like 'get over it', thoughtless encouragement like 'You've still got Yamada and Suzuki, right?' and the usual slogan of 'don't be so timid'.

Second, he tried to force his own convictions onto others. What were the convictions that he was operating from? "Boys from the judo club should always walk with their heads held high." "Men are not meant to cry or show fear." "This situation can be improved if we work hard enough."

These kinds of convictions are a product of someone's education or their experiences or cultural values; they're very much restricted to the individual, so it doesn't make sense to try to universalize them and force them onto everyone. And even if you could push them onto others, that would rob them of their own individual convictions.

Third, there is an aspect of trying to have the other person depend on you. Wanatabe doesn't normally come into contact with junior students, so why is he suddenly in a hurry to start training again? Is he just trying to interfere? Maybe it was merely to satisfy his desire to play the part of the senior student again.

How do you think the juniors would have felt after having been told "shut up and follow me"? Do you think they would have been glad to have run into a senior who was kind and concerned about them? Or would they find it unpleasant, being forced to get on with their training without having been able to straighten out their feelings first?

At any rate, pulling rank and interfering just because he was in a senior position–and the juniors not being able to refuse just because they're in a junior position–bears all the hallmarks of an unhealthy dependent relationship. You can see this kind of 'wet' relationship, based on acting out of feelings of obligation, throughout Japanese society.

The ideal mentor

Watanabe's story is a parody of the 'road to Emmaeus' story that you find in Luke 24:13-35. This time Jesus does not say 'come and follow me,' but he approaches the disciples and walks along with them. Then he asks them, "What are these matters you are discussing so intently as you walk along?"

He must have known what they were talking about. So why did he ask? Perhaps his question was giving them an opportunity to talk. He didn't start off the encounter by screaming 'you idiots!' at them. Listening to the other person while showing sympathy with their feelings is the fundamental attitude of a mentor.

Then, with a gloomy expression, they replied "Are you the only visitor to Jerusalem who doesn't know the things that have happened there in these days?" There's an anger lurking beneath that question. Maybe it's the anger of someone who has had their expectations betrayed. Sometimes people who are hurting will lash out at those who are trying to support them. From the mentor's point of view, this is unfair and illogical treatment.

When the juniors expressed unwarranted anger at Watanabe in the above story, he tried to protect himself by getting angry back at them. But Jesus faced up to the disciples' anger, and then asked them to go on: "What things?" Maybe as the disciples spoke from their own experiences, they re-experienced the emotions that they had felt at the time. Once again, Jesus's approach is not one of confrontation, but one of support and acceptance.

However, once the disciples had finished their long story, Jesus challenges them anew. With this challenge, the disciples' feelings are not offended, nor are their characters bruised. We can surmise this from the fact that the disciples afterwards reflected, "didn't our hearts burn within us while he was speaking with us on the road, while he was explaining the scriptures to us?"

Jesus himself explained from the whole Bible the suffering and resurrection of the Christ. As he was presenting the truth to them, Jesus corrected their mistaken thinking and the attitude of their hearts, helped them to understand the truth, and consequently prepared them to stand as witnesses to the resurrection.

When the party reached their destination at the village, Jesus appeared to be going on further. The disciples had to work at it to get Jesus to stop and have a meal with them. Maybe Jesus was hurrying to some other business. Immediately after his resurrection, Jesus should have had no more important work than putting the finishing touches on the preparation to send his disciples into the world.

Whatever the reason, we can surmise that Jesus gave his disciples the chance to confess that their hearts were stirred and that they wanted to know more and to grow more. This is what determines the success or failure of mentoring: a voluntary declaration of intent. They have to want it. Jesus did not say "follow me", or try to force himself upon them. Instead, the disciples thought they had to work so that they could continue to be with him.

The curtain closes on this episode with Jesus's disappearance. Even though their mentor had gone away, the disciples returned to Jerusalem with joy, and began the work of witnessing. This is the goal of mentoring: not that the mentee comes to depend upon the mentor, but that even if the mentor goes away, the mentee can stand on their own two feet, recognise the personal call that has been placed upon their life, and carry it out with joy. We'll look at this more in the next chapter.

The balance between support and challenge

Jesus' mentoring on the Emmaeus road maintains a balance between support and challenge. If the mentor only gives support, without giving the challenge to improve, there is a danger that the mentee will end up remaining a spiritual infant. Conversely, if the mentor only challenges without thinking about the mentee's circumstances and without giving any emotional support, the mentee may well end up getting burnt out. What we are looking for is mentoring that understands the other person's situation, remembers one's own tendencies, maintains a balance, and follows God's guidance.

The father of the bride

Bringing up the bride to love
Christ wholeheartedly

A preacher loses his bearings

For ten years, I devoted myself to being a faithful interpreter of the Bible. I thought that if the truth wasn't proclaimed in church, then there's nowhere else for people to hear the truth... As well as, obviously, the Sunday sermon, I prepared messages for the weekday Bible studies with all my heart and all my mind. For the womens' group, I put together a set of study series so that they could study the Bible systematically. This was because I was aware that the job of enabling the faithful to correctly understand and apply the Bible was the vocation that had been given to me as a preacher.

These days I still put everything I've got into teaching the Bible, but recently, I'm starting to become unsure whether my sermons really have the power to change the lives of the members of the congregation. I say this because the other day I went to hear a lecture. It had been a long time since I had had to sit through someone else's lecture, and do you know what? It was really, really boring.

Since I came out of Bible college, I had always been the one speaking; I'd hardly ever been the one sitting down for such a long time to listen to someone else.

Now of course, a lecture and a sermon have different content, but they're similar because they both involve one person talking in a monologue for a long time. I realised that even if my sermon content was moving and impressive, having to concentrate on listening to someone else for half an hour to an hour is seriously hard work. When I thought that, I was filled with gratitude towards those church members who patiently listened to me even through my more dry sermons.

Looking back, I think that I was so afraid of making a mistake in my sermon content that I didn't pay enough attention to how those listening would receive it. Even if the sermon is correct, if the congregation are bored out of their minds then we're both wasting our time. What is the point of the congregation dragging their tired bodies to a Sunday service in order to hear a 'boring lecture'–and then go home even more tired?

More fundamentally, even if one could expound doctrine clearly and correctly, the big question is what effect it has on the lives of the believers. Now if the pastor just can't teach, that's one issue, but more than that, I ended up thinking, if it were Jesus, what would he do? Would he fill his disciples' heads with doctrinal knowledge? Wouldn't he do something else instead?

The mentor as surrogate parent

A confession like that makes us ask an important question about church structure: "Is God really looking for the lecture-type of service or meeting?" How many people really come to church thinking that they want to study more about God? I think probably more people think that studying is what they did when they were at school. We don't want to turn into someone who "boxes like one who hits only air", (1 Corinthians 9:26) so we need to be aware of what people's real needs are.

So what are people actually looking for when they come to church? According to Nobuo Tanaka, a pastor and counsellor, most people in Japan come to church to find a parent figure.

This is part of an interview with him:

> In thirty years, not one person has, to be honest, come to me for a real consultation. It might look like a consultation, but in reality they are looking to me as a substitute father or surrogate mother. So no matter how much I show them the solutions, it's a waste of time. The consultation is a formality or an excuse to meet me; really what they come seeking is not a solution to their pain, but they come seeking love.

In other words, many people coming to the church see the pastor or pastors' wife as a surrogate parent, and come unconsciously seeking the acceptance that they did not receive from their physical parents or caregivers. If this is true, the church needs to support them not through teaching but through relationships. To shut hurting people into a classroom and make them study is as irrelevant an approach as scratching the feet of someone with an itchy back. People looking for a parent figure must have their immediate needs met before they can receive the knowledge of a true heavenly Father who accepts them unconditionally.

Mentors, whether they be clergy or lay, have been given the job of bridging the gap and leading these people to a new parent-child relationship with their heavenly Father. It may be necessary for these mentees to go through a phase of accepting another person as their substitute parent.

For people from a broken home, with a negative image of what it is to be a father, it is difficult to get across a healthy image of their heavenly Father with words alone. First, the mentor accepts the wounded person, builds up a trust relationship with them, and through their own lifestyle of trusting and obeying their heavenly Father, we hope to make visible the invisible heavenly Father. This is the application of Jesus' incarnational principle of "He who has seen me has seen the Father" to pastoring.

The danger of codependency

There is a huge risk when the mentor functions as a foster parent for quite a period of time. This is the risk that both the mentor and the injured person end up forming an unhealthy relationship. The relationship that two Japanese people form together is essentially a mutual dependency relationship with one taking a 'parent' role and the other taking a 'child' role. So unless one is particularly careful, the mentor ends up not producing a disciple of Christ, but rather producing his own disciple. The role of the mentor as a foster parent is, as much as possible, to hand over people to their true heavenly Father.

There are two ways in which mentoring can descend into a codependency relationship. The first is that the mentee starts to want to depend upon the mentor. When the mentee is satisfied with human relationships within a pseudo-family, they want to remain there. It is natural for those who have experienced family break-down, but then come across the tenderness that they have been looking for, to always want to remain within that intimate relationship with the mentor.

But as long as they remain there, they cannot enter into a one-to-one personal relationship with their heavenly Father. The mentor must point out that the destination point of their search for a father figure is when they are embraced in the bosom of the Father and Creator.

Another danger has its roots in unsolved issues within the mentor themselves. In particular, there can be a tendency for the mentor to want a dependence relationship where 'I give him help and he relies on me.' If someone who is still searching for a parent figure themselves starts trying to mentoring others, they end up using the mentoring relationship for their own self-confirmation, self-worth and self-actualization.

Of course there is a sense in which those who mentor others will themselves grow, (Galatians 6:6), but if that becomes the goal, they will not end up helping the mentee. Instead, there is the danger that the relationship will hinder the mentee's independence.

Preparing the bride of Christ

The mentor is like a father bringing up a bride. "For I am jealous for you with godly jealousy, because I promised you in marriage to one husband, to present you as a pure virgin to Christ." (2 Corinthians 11:2).

One condition for the mentee to enter into that intimate relationship with God, symbolised in the Bible as marriage to Christ, is independence from the mentor. Just as the bride cannot bring her father with her into the new household, the mentee must have the determination to stand alone before God. In the same way, the mentor cannot keep the bride at his side forever; for the bride belongs 'to one husband'.

In the first stages of mentoring, it may be helpful to avoid a mutual dependency relationship by beginning to pray together whilst imagining the mentee being able to leave the mentoring relationship and stand on their own two feet in their walk with God. To bring up the bride to love not the mentor, but Christ alone, is to consider the heart of God for the mentee.

The trainer is in the process of being trained

The following table shows how the trainer is themselves in the process of being trained.

	Mentee	Worker	Main approach	Risk	Countermeasure
Stage 1	Seeking a parent	Foster parent	Acceptance and Support	Co-dependency	Commitment to God the True Father
Stage 2	Seeking a universal dependency partner	Father of the bride	Teaching and challenge	Regression	Celebration
Stage 3	Foster parent to another	Friend	Encouraging and resourcing	Loss of confidence	Catching the vision

In the first stage, the mentor relates as a foster parent to the mentee who is looking for a parent figure. The main approaches here are acceptance and support.

It is necessary to be aware of the risk of a co-dependent relationship, but it is possible to avoid that by continually reaffirming our allegiance to God as our true Father.

The second stage is one where the mentor functions as the "father of the bride." The mentor teaches from the Bible about how God is our father and is the ultimately-dependable partner, and the mentor also challenges the mentee in ways that will bring them to ultimate trust in God. If this challenge is not present during this stage, we may observe the mentee regressing towards wanting to stay in the relationship with the visible mentor. However, as the mentee celebrates the grace of God that they have been experiencing, they will be able to turn their thoughts towards having an intimate relationship with God for themselves.

In the third stage, the mentee himself begins work as the foster parent figure to another person. The original mentor acts as a friend, and provides resources for the mentee to grow as a new mentor themselves. The new mentor may run into problems while teaching another person, and this may lead to a loss of confidence, but the original mentor can encourage them by refocusing them on their vision of becoming a person who helps others to grow.

The mentor's independence: Responding to God's love

Guiding others to stand
independently before God

Deciding for yourself before God

"We're not trying to push our own vision and values onto you two. God has his own individual plan appropriate to each one of those He has chosen. Our wish is to see God accomplishing that plan through your lives, and we want to do anything we can to make that happen. We'll even do the babysitting if you need it."

This is what a couple of friends said to Mr and Mrs. Sawamura. And, true to their word, whenever they visited, they would gently take the baby from Mrs. Sawamura and babysit for them, and together would help the couple to confirm the calling God had for them.

Since Mr. Sawamura was a sports-minded person, he was initially at a loss with their style of training; he expected to have all the answers presented to him up-front. The teaching he had received up to this point was essentially just being told (and compelled) what to do, and so he perhaps felt a little irritated. But as the mentoring progressed, he learnt how to decide things for himself before God.

Mr. Sawamura remembers it this way. "If they had come right out and told us, either directly or indirectly, what we ought to be doing, then it would have been difficult for us to own the vision for ourselves. Because they respected our personality and took things at our pace, and waited until we could get hold of God's heart for ourselves, I was able to understand what my Heavenly Father thinks about me. Not that anyone taught me, but I was able to hear it from God for myself. There is no greater joy than this."

He said that he had never experienced this kind of coaching from his parents or schoolteachers or sports club coaches. "I was quite happy to be told what to do and to do it, without needing to think or decide anything for myself, but I ended up neglecting my own responsibility. If I did exactly what I was told and it didn't work out right, I could blame it on the instructor. But if I decide it myself, I have to take on the consequences of that action. Cutting myself away from dependency upon an instructor is a big challenge, but I think that

through doing it, I've been able to feel close to God as
He helped me on the way."

Dependence or independence

The mentors helped Mr. and Mrs. Sawamura to be
independent before God. However, independence does
not mean totally ceasing to rely upon others. If Mrs.
Sawamura had not entrusted her baby to one of their
mentors, they might never have been able to come
calmly before God. Trusting the mentor and being
comfortable in accepting any help that is necessary is
a skill needed for healthy interpersonal growth. You
could say that it was precisely because they were able
to do that, that they learnt how to stand on their own
two feet before God.

Dependence is not a bad thing in itself. If someone
is not able to build relationships which include space
for dependence, they become isolated. Each of us has
been created with a need for other people.

The real question is working out the boundaries of
our own responsibility. We are seeking to develop an
attitude which can go ahead and accept help where help
is necessary, and where the other person can joyfully
give help, but which avoids violating the boundaries of
responsibility.

In Mr. and Mrs. Sawamura's mentoring, accepting
the offer of childminding was an area where they could

rightly depend on others, but understanding and accepting God's will for them was something they could not have delegated. When God was telling Abram about the reward that He would give him in the future, God took Abram alone outside and said to him "Look up at the heavens and count the stars–if indeed you can count them. So shall your offspring be." (Genesis 15:5) Only God and Abram appear in this scene. There was no compulsion or force.

There are things which God wants to say to us as individuals. Like Mary, who "sat at the Lord's feet listening to what he said" (Luke 10:39), it is our own responsibility to leave behind the things of the day and listen intently to what the Lord has to say to us.

If the mentor didn't just do the babysitting but also went on to say "your vision is such-and-such", then even if what they said had been correct, the Sawamuras would have missed the opportunity to hear God for themselves. When the mentor steps over the bounds of their responsibility in order to support someone, the mentee is no longer able to voluntarily react to God's call, possess the vision for themselves, or experience the richness of fellowship with God.

The mentor is not someone who comes up with the right answers all by themselves, but someone who helps the mentee be able to stand up on their own two feet before God.

The temptation to show off your abilities

Incidentally, why do you think those who mentored the Sawamuras used this style of mentoring? It's because there is a hidden tendency within mentors to want people to depend on them from the outset. According to Shinya Maruya, there is a tendency in our society to teach someone not to be independent, but to be reliant on the leader.

What's the advantage for the leader in having someone depend upon them? The advantage is that you get an opportunity to demonstrate that your knowledge is worth depending upon.

This tendency to want to show off your own abilities is not limited to Japanese, but is omnipresent. The first temptation that our Lord experienced in the wilderness played on this very tendency. (Luke 4:3)

There are times when the church as the body of Christ gets tempted in the same way. Whenever we begin to worry about what people think of our work, or how rapidly our church is growing, or how much our ministry has accomplished, or how many people we support or "get saved", we fall into this same temptation.

"Do you love me?"

To overcome this temptation, Henri Nouwen suggests asking yourself the following question:

> "Do you love me?" This question should be asked at the core of all our Christian labor. It is this question alone which makes us into servants of the Lord, not seeking for our own glory, and at the same time, in a very real sense, makes us into people of confidence.

If the mentor, entrusted with Jesus' flock, is to participate in the glorious work of helping their growth, he or she needs to be be able to reply to the Lord's question, "Yes, Lord, you know that I love you." Mentoring, with the single desire of seeing people totally satisfied with the love of the crucified Christ, and witnessing with their whole lives to God's unconditional love, cannot be done for any selfish motive.

Only by continuing to stand alone before the question "Do you love me?" can the mentor work as a disciple of Christ, who sacrificed his own life so that others could live.

The church: a fellowship serving one another

Serving each other as the priesthood of all believers

'Willing to go the extra mile'

One day, Mrs. A, realising the importance of intercessory prayer, decided that every day she would lift up the names of a number of people in prayer. She started by writing out a list of all the people that she wanted to intercede for, but thought that such a mechanical way of doing things didn't really feel like it was coming from the heart, so she tried to memorise the list of names and their prayer requests. Over the course of year, the list of names in her head grew until eventually it passed two hundred people. To get through this kind of a list, even with very brief prayers, took over an hour. But she was someone of great stickability, and continued this practice without fail even when she was ill or on holiday.

Eventually, when she was no longer able to recite the whole list from memory, she became irritable and unable to sleep. After around five years, she developed symptoms similar to a mild mental illness. She would get annoyed if one of her children spoke to her while she was praying, because if someone spoke to her she would not be able to remember how far she had got through her list. If she was busy and unable to 'clear' more than half her list by the end of the day, she would take out her bad mood on her husband.

Looking back on that time, she says, "even though at the start it was fun to pray for people I loved, eventually it became quite hard work. I was calling on God, but my heart was empty. I was even aware myself that it had become a dull and boring work, but I was afraid to give up something that I'd continued for so many years. I carried on that way for eight years."

If she had not undergone mentoring, perhaps she would have set a new world record in this 'work'. But when the mentor began to probe for whose benefit exactly she was doing this praying, she was able to realise that she was doing it for her own sense of safety and pride. Prayer, which is meant to be fellowship with God, had been swapped for a 'magic spell', a psychological crutch. Through mentoring, she learnt to live a lifestyle of listening to God's voice and rejoicing in the freedom of the Holy Spirit. It is not too much to say that her family relationships were also transformed for the better.

Not willing to go the extra mile

There are those who are willing to go the extra mile, like Mrs. A, who struggle through even to places far beyond God's leading for them. These people face the temptation of preferring the satisfaction of achieving something by their own efforts to receiving God's affirmation of them.

Then, by contrast to Mrs. A, there are those who have no confidence in themselves and who are not willing to go the extra mile. They have a tendency to get caught up in a vicious circle because they end up seeing themselves as 'sinful'.

Mrs. B was worried that she had not been able to do her devotions for many years. If she got up early and opened her Bible, she would soon find herself dozing off. She'd been a Christian for twenty years. This condition had been going on for ten of them. But she was still upset that she could not perform her morning devotions.

When she went to a conference she would get a 'spiritual shot in the arm' and be able to do it for a few days, but after a week or so once again she would get out her Bible and nod off. It always started well but she was unable to keep it going, and she fell into the vicious circle of cursing her own weak-willed spirit.

Even someone like that was changed by being mentored. Her image of devotions consisted of singing a hymn, reading the Bible, reflecting on the word, understanding its meaning, thinking about how to apply it to her life, and finally offering thanks and intercession and personal prayer needs. To get through all this would take at least thirty minutes.

But the mentor, instead of challenging her to go straight into a thirty-minute devotion, suggested that she start with three minutes. The contents would go like this: In the first minute, stilling her heart and turning it towards God, saying 'I am waiting for you. I welcome your presence.' In the second minute, she would think over her favourite passage in Isaiah, 'you are precious in my sight,' and say 'Lord, you really love me that much, don't you?' The final minute was spent thinking over the things that she had to be thankful for, and saying 'thank you' to God.

She thought that if that was all there was to it, she could probably manage it. Encouraged by the mentor, she gave it a go, and was able to keep it up. As her devotional time naturally began to lengthen, she introduced several variations into the content.

Mrs. B explains it this way. 'Now when I get up in the morning, I feel like I want to talk to Jesus. And I know that there are things that Jesus wants to talk with me about. There are times when my first hour of the morning is a private date with Jesus, and times when it's a strategy meeting.'

As well as accepting Mrs. B's weakness, the mentor suggested a next step that she felt that she was able to take. Personal growth takes time. Basic strength and speed of development varies from person to person. As well as knowing the individual, you need to adopt a patient and flexible approach.

The keywords: 'One another'

Confessing sins to one another, forgiving one another, accepting one another, loving one another, praying for one another, encouraging one another, instructing one another, serving one another. Not merely the 'religious professionals,' but the whole body of believers can serve one another as priests. We can all bear each others' responsibilities so that each person can be transformed into the likeness of Christ.

If you think of mentoring as some set of interpersonal skills for motivating another person, you might not expect much in the way of transformation, even if you apply this to the specialised field of church growth and discipleship. But if even just one person can confess their hidden weaknesses boldly in front of others, and humbly say 'please pray for me,' then there's a possibility that the whole church can begin to develop a spirit of serving one another.

Many people, even if they keep up the appearance of having no problems at all, are looking for a safe place where they can share the sufferings and questions in their hearts. We all need friends who help us as we take responsibility for our own growth, to challenge us and focus us on the call of God.

Brought up in fellowship

Restoration of relationships
in communion with God

The bonds of marriage

Some years back, three groups of pastors and their wives went on a retreat in a mountain reservation. Let's introduce the thoughts of one of the wives who attended.

Before the retreat, all the attendees made a promise that we would, as a rule, not talk about our church or our children. We would only talk about personal growth, spiritual growth, or about our marital relationship. When I heard this, I thought 'if you take out the church and our children from our conversation, what on earth is going to be left?' We had never done this sort of thing since getting married, and of course not before we were married. That was how our conversations were inclined.

In the first part of the program, we spent the time until the evening meal alone as a couple. It had been many years since we were able to spend time by ourselves, away from children and church people. As we walked, I was overcome with gratitude to God for allowing me to share my life with the partner that he had given me.

Until that point, since I was under the impression that I should serve wholeheartedly and devotedly, even sacrificing my family, I was always aware of people's gaze upon me, and I couldn't imagine having relaxed time as a couple.

But this time, although it was a little awkward at first, I was able to experience the comfort of loving my husband and being loved by him. Rather than just being a 'pastor's wife', it was a delightful thing for me to see that I was the wife of this particular man.

Her husband says this:

When we went for that walk, I was able to see her not as my co-worker, or as the mother of our children, but as a woman, and my heart was so full of love for my wife that I wanted to cry out, 'this one is at last bone of my bones and flesh of my flesh'. It was a short time, but that time that I spent as a couple with my wife shone with the freshness of a honeymoon. We think of that experience as a new start for us.

Healing relationships

That retreat also had time for mentoring of each couple by the others, and fellowship between the pastors' wives.

> After dinner, the two older couples listened intently to us. Through answering their questions, we were able to understand how a couple can help each other in their growth. I was a little nervous to start with, but I was gradually able to relax in the warmth of the environment. I felt that they accepted us, not as people with the title of 'pastor' and 'pastor's wife', but just as we were.

On the second day, just the pastors' wives had a time of talking together.

> Even though our workplaces were different, it was a relief to talk to people in the same position as me. I enjoyed the beautiful nature, the delicious food and the close fellowship of friends, and my body and soul were both refreshed.

Only in an open environment of mutual acceptance can we get rid of the 'unseen armour' we use to protect ourselves. That kind of environment can bring about the healing of relationships with those closest to us. When we place ourselves at peace in the fellowship of those that God has given us, God demonstrates through those relationships his astonishing power of healing and reconciliation. (1 John 4:16) Fellowship with the

Father and the Son can revive authentic relationships between husband and wife, parent and child, brother and sister, friend and neighbour.

Mentoring is God's work

Mentoring is not merely a technique for personal development, but it is one aspect of the communion of the saints. God's desire for each person to be developed is realized through warm fellowship, freed from pride and captivity. Through the work of mentors arrayed throughout the body of Christ, the Father himself embraces, grows and guides those receiving mentoring, so that they grow up and 'be transformed into his image' (2 Corinthians 3:18)

For instance, suppose someone is really impressed with the idea of mentoring, and decides to start mentoring someone else. He believes that God wants to bring about growth in a particular person, and dreams of seeing them blossom into their full potential. So before the first mentoring session, he prays like this: 'Father, I have prepared long and hard. I've even prayed for hours on end for this person. You know well how much I want be to useful for you. I want to give this whole work over to you. Please accept me and my ministry.'

I wonder if our heavenly Father, hearing this sort of prayer, might think something like this: 'I already accept you because my son died in your place. You do not need to labour for my acceptance. Developing people is not your work, but mine. I will take responsibility for it and I will do it.

So don't give your work over to me, but rather put it to one side. If you do that, then I can fill you and minister grace and truth to him, and then you will see what works I will do through you!'

As long as we persist in a pattern of prayer that sets out our own plans before God and asks Him to bless them, we cannot experience the grace of God working within us. Mentoring is a process where God Himself develops people as they experience His love, and mentoring is the sign of a healthy community. Although as a discipline it involves many strategic concepts, it is fundamentally about the sovereignty of God rejoicing in us and presencing Himself within trust relationships. "So neither the one who plants counts for anything, nor the one who waters, but God who causes the growth." (1 Corinthians 3:7)

Being allowed to participate in God's work

There was a pastor who loved gardening. One day as he was working, his young son said 'I'm going to help too!' and came into the garden. So they began to garden together, but the boy treated the plants so roughly that sorting them out after him meant that everything took twice as long. When they had finished everything, the boy ran back into the house and said to his mother 'I did it all!' But the man said to his friends later, 'I really enjoyed working in the garden with my son'.

Does our heavenly Father really need the help of His children? He is the person who caused the world to come into existence just with one word. Perhaps there are times when we try to help but actually we cause a lot of trouble. But since God enjoys working with us, in His mercy He invites us to help, and so we also can enjoy working with Him. In the middle of a loving fellowship focused on Him, we can take part in the exciting work of developing others.

Listening is loving

*A listener is a lightning rod
for the other's emotions*

The first step of mentoring

I'd like you to imagine a café run by an owner who loves lemon tea, and who thinks that lemon tea is better than everything else. He doesn't bother to come over to the customers and take their order, but brings them cups of lemon tea as though it were the most natural thing in the world. Even if they manage to order tea with milk, they get lemon tea. This man has no ill intentions. It's just that he honestly believes that lemon tea is the best way of appreciating tea, and he is convinced that his customers will be happiest if they're drinking lemon tea. Is this café going to flourish?

When serving customers in a café, the first thing the waiter will do is say, 'what would you like?' In much the same way, the first step of mentoring is also to take in what the other person is saying, and to hear and understand their thoughts and feelings. If you speak merely from your own opinions or areas of interest, you will not only fail to understand the other person, but will also lose their trust as their mentor.

In Proverbs 18:13, it says "The one who gives an answer before he listens—that is his folly and his shame," and James commands "Let every person be quick to listen, slow to speak, slow to anger." (James 1:19) The Bible teaches us to listen before speaking. Maybe the reason God gave us one mouth and two ears was so that we could listen twice as much as we speak.

I want my story to be heard

Most people feel that they want their story to be heard. The other day I saw the movie 'What Women Want.' In this love story set in a Chicago advertising agency, Nick, the character played by Mel Gibson, has an accident and is able to hear the internal thoughts of women. One day, he listens to the heart of his rival Darcy (played by Helen Hunt) and gets to know what she is really like. She is a strong career woman who does not show her weaknesses in front of others, and always pretends to be on top of everything, but is actually delicate, easily hurt and carrying the burden of a lonely past. The Japanese advertising copy ran 'I want you to listen to the heart beneath my suit.' I thought 'it's not just women who want to be listened to!'

Two years ago I had the opportunity to interview a very successful leader in business evangelism. He said that the biggest need that businessmen have is for a private, trusting environment where they can have their stories heard. Many men are exhausted in the middle of a prolonged recession, but neither their families, nor their companies, nor their neighbours can understand the cries of their hearts.

Learning to listen

But while most people want their story to be heard, they don't necessarily want to hear others! So they pretend that they're listening, and then end up talking about their own greatness or their own unhappinesses. To stop this from happening, one needs not only to have the kind of love that puts the other person's benefit first, but also to get a grip of basic listening skills.

Since many people who are hurting have a mistaken understanding of themselves or of their circumstances, the listener must objectively point out this misunderstanding. This is where the mentor needs patience. If you point out the flaw before the person has realised it themselves, you end up creating dependency in the other person, and they do not take charge of their own development. You must not steal the opportunity for them to find the right answer and decide to put it into practice for themselves.

Furthermore, many people already know what is the best thing for them to do. Their actual problem is either a lack of certainty in taking the course which they already know to be correct, or a fear of the consequences of their decision.

For instance, if someone is saying 'I can't forgive that person,' then teaching them 'you must forgive' is likely to be counterproductive, since they are already thinking somewhere in their heart, 'if I can, I want to forgive.' The job of the mentor is to imagine a situation where the other person can think nothing other than 'I cannot forgive,' and then to try to understand that kind of distress; without preaching, without judging, without threatening, without inciting, but taking notice of the other person's feelings. And when you have found those feelings, to tenderly sympathise with them. To understand if the other person is angry or sadly or lonely or irritated or depressed or holds feelings of inferiority, and to reflect those emotions.

For example, saying to someone who is angry 'it really makes you mad, doesn't it?' In short, this is 'rejoicing with those who rejoice, weeping with those who weep.' (Romans 12:15) Continuing to accept the feelings of hurting people prepares the way for the next challenging stage of 'speaking the truth in love.' (Ephesians 4:15)

Through the mentor's 'lifestyle of listening', people have the opportunity to experience the touch of Christ's love. Robert Logan says that 'mentoring is not the skill of giving the right answers, but the skill of asking the right questions.' I recommend that, when you feel that you want to give away the answer, you ask a question which allows the other person to find the answer for themselves. Jesus taught his disciples by asking them the right questions. (c.f. Matthew 16:15)

By asking good questions, you can make judgements about the circumstances that the other person finds themselves in, encourage them to think seriously about the issues that they should be examining, and help them to make important decisions.

The mentor as a lightning rod

About ten years ago, I was able to ask Dr. Masumi Toyotome, an advocate of the Nameless Movement about the approach that she had pioneered called "the evangelism of the ear." I asked her "what percent of an interview time should be spent in listening?", and she replied "Listen for at least 90% of the time." When I said "I can't do that," she replied "But listening is fun!" Since she was smiling while she said it, I came to think "maybe listening can be fun..."

The listener is like a lightning rod who takes on the speaker's grumbling or anger or whatever emotions they have stored up. But if they're then stored up in you, wouldn't you burn out? By earthing them through you—that is, by passing them on from you to Jesus—both you and the other person are protected.

I realised recently that when Dr. Toyotome said that listening could be fun, maybe she was hinting at the depth of relationship with God that she cultivated through listening to others.

Celebrating seeing God's truth

The good mentor is a friend who discovers God's good work

The power of words of affirmation

In the church where I used to work, we had a teaching course that we called a 'self-discovery seminar.' The main aim of this was, through teaching people to write their personal history, to help them to discover their gifts and their calling.

While I was talking with a woman in her late fifties, something unexpected happened. Reading her personal history in advance, I could see that her life had been a string of hardships, but in spite of that, she was trying really hard to live a positive life. So when the interview started, I said, 'reading your personal history, I realised that you've really been giving it all you've got.'

Immediately I said that, she broke down into floods of tears. There was no way I could have predicted that something like that would happen, particularly since I knew that she didn't exactly think very much of me. However, since that day she has become a great source of understanding and support for me and my ministry, and I have found that she has wanted more and more to serve the Lord and serve others.

This incident taught me a lesson. An encouraging word, just a single word, can really change someone's heart. I didn't go in with the intention of encouraging her, but rather I said the first thing that I felt and God used that word of affirmation.

Let's celebrate!

The goal of mentoring is to help someone to be able to live a life appropriate to the Gospel. So even if they think 'now is not the time' or 'I just don't want to do it', we speak with love about 'what ought to be' and encourage them to wrestle with the issues. However, we have to begin by recognising the good things that God has already given to them and the good work that He has already accomplished in them, thanking God and celebrating together.

A good mentor is a friend who discovers the good works that God has already begun inside the other person. "Whatever is true, whatever is worthy of respect, whatever is just, whatever is pure, whatever is lovely, whatever is commendable, if something is excellent or praiseworthy, think about these things." (Phillipians 4:8) If they think about that and try to keep it in their hearts, they will be able to find what they are looking for.

For instance, until my eldest son got hold of a little car with the strange name of 'Toppo', I didn't even notice that there was such a car. However, now that I know that there is, I see this make of car all the time on the roads. Since our attention is selective, being conscious of something allows us to see things that we didn't see before.

If for example there isn't as much development as expected while mentoring, if you are able to think 'well, there has been a little bit of progress', you can recognise that as God's work and celebrate in it. For instance, I don't think there are many fathers who, when their toddler makes a few steps and falls over, would get angry and say 'Why did you fall?' Wouldn't they rather focus not on the falling but praise the walking, and celebrate their child's development? Even if the child didn't walk at all, but showed the will to walk, wouldn't the father watch with smiling face?

My face is...beautiful?

The world is full of negative words. The other day I met a young mother who was loudly scolding her little boy in an elevator. She was saying over and over 'I don't need children who do that kind of thing!' She got so angry that it hurt me as I was standing next to them.

Even in the home we fire around 'messages that deny our existence.' Our schools and communities and companies (and possibly even our churches) brim over with these negative messages. I don't know who studied it, but I've heard it said that 95% of our newspapers are made up of negative words.

I personally suffered from a great many insecurities. I used to hate my face and my body, and be disillusioned with my abilities and my personality. I think it was in my early teens that I went to a certain camp and was looking after some younger children, when one of them said to me 'your eyes look like a fox's!' After that, I found it impossible to accept myself and my own face, and I used to have to pretend to look happy.

It was only in my thirties that I was freed from this complex. I was living in America, and a Korean friend said to me, 'I love my own slitty eyes, flat features, thin hair, yellow skin and round body!' He was a good friend, but however favourably you looked at him you couldn't really say he was handsome, so I thought this was surprising when I heard it. And then he said 'Because I love God who made me this way.' This immediately blew away my inferiority complex towards white people.

No matter who tells you that you are worthless, God says to you that 'your voice is sweet, and your face is lovely.' (Song of Solomon 2:14) The affirming words of a mentor focus people on the truth that our lives are the 'workmanship' (Ephesians 2:10) of God, the master craftsman. God does not want us to suffer from insecurities caused by comparing ourselves to other people, but He wants us to accept who we are with thanksgiving.

The Psalmist says 'The boundary lines have fallen for me in pleasant places; surely I have a delightful inheritance.' (Psalm 16:6, NIV) The Psalmist can write that the boundaries that he has been assigned are 'pleasant places' based on a faith that believes in the personality and power of God who always gives us 'a delightful inheritance.' He is not thinking that his own land is delightful in comparison to other people's. When we can confess that our inheritance is a 'pleasant place', we well up with a joy and excitement that the world cannot imagine.

Jesus' viewpoint

When Jesus was told by God 'you are my one dear Son; in you I take great delight,' he had not yet taught a thing about the kingdom of God. He had not healed one sick person or driven out one evil spirit or helped one poor person or taught his disciples anything. But despite all that, God said to him from heaven, 'I'm glad that you're here.'

We can learn at least two things from this passage. The first is that our Father is saying the same thing to us who he bought with His Son's blood. The other is that receiving unconditional love is the precondition to all good works. One day Jesus looked straight at Simon and said to him 'You will be called Cephas (rock)'. (John

1:42) What Jesus saw was not Peter's present situation but the potential and possibilities inside him and the plan that God had for him. The job of the mentor is to focus from Jesus' point of view on the truth of God who wants to take responsibility for the other person's life and lead it forward, and to rejoice in that.

Keeping focus on the most important things

A torture situation

In 1997, I had dinner with Robert Logan, a specialist in leadership development, and he said to me, 'you work too hard. You try to do too many things.' But to be honest, I didn't really take that warning very seriously. At the time if someone told me 'you're so busy,' I would take it as almost a perverse compliment.

A few years later, I received the same warning from another person. After listening to me for a while, he said 'you're like someone who is being tortured. It's as if your hands and feet are bound and your body is being pulled apart by horses.' Certainly at the time I was kept very busy with all the work piling up before my eyes, and I was putting off being still before God or enjoying time with my family. But even so, I thought it was impossible to set aside the responsibilities that I had and the work in which I found so much fulfillment. This was my excuse: "This job and that job is the work that God has given to me. I can't give up on it half-way through."

When I said that, he started to tell me his own story. "Until a few years ago, I used to think like you do. Since I was proud of my work, even if someone warned me to reconsider my priorities, I thought it was a waste of time. Just like you, two separate friends warned me about this, but at the time I didn't have ears to hear. What do you think happened as a result? All of a sudden, God took away from me all of the work that I thought was so important. It was a big shock for me then. But now I know that because that happened, I can enjoy the grace I have now."

That was a very persuasive story. From that time, I began to pray seriously that I would be able to change my lifestyle.

Fighting to change how I used my time

I then decided to gradually change how I used my time. To change this long-established pattern of 'all work and no play,' I needed careful preparation. I got to grips with concrete objectives of increasing the amount of time spent on various things by a certain number of percent.

What I wanted to increase was the time I spent on fellowship with God and fellowship with others. Even if I accomplished something, if I couldn't celebrate that achievement with God and with my family and with my friends, what would be the point? I decided to use my time to build up my relationship with God who loved me and to build up my relationships with the important people around me.

But to start something new, you need to give up something you're already doing and reserve the time it took. So I decided to restrict the time that I used for research, writing and lecturing. Just as I made that decision, almost as if to test my willpower, I got several impressive offers of work that up until then I would not have thought twice before accepting. It was hard to refuse these offers from people who had been kind to me in the past, and I worried that if I just refused everything, people would soon forget about me.

But despite that, the reason I was able to say 'no' was because of some encouragement from above. God rejoiced in my determination, no matter how small it was, and I gradually learned that the things that I chose were clearly more important than the things that I gave up.

For instance, my devotions used to be a one-way conversation, like someone who hangs up the phone just after saying what he wants to say. But when I gave the initiative over to God and was able to secure time every morning purely enjoying fellowship with God, I was able to understand how much God looked forward to that time.

Fellowship with God, fellowship with others

The thing that changed most was the way I used to spend Saturdays. I used to work the whole year around without holidays, but now from Saturday morning to just after noon I go out on a date with my wife. Then when we get back, from 1 to 1:30, we have a silent time of 'weekly retreat.' Through that I can catch hold of the plans that God has for my life and what he wants to do through my life, and put my own thoughts in order and align them with the thoughts of God. Generally I cry like a baby as I am touched by the love of God. When this is over, I make dinner for the family. This is a practical expression of my love for my wife and children.

However recently we've often been setting aside the whole Saturday, morning to evening, as a day of prayer, and so I've felt it has been necessary to find a separate time to have together with my wife. On weekdays, I've arranged to have regular time for fellowship with staff and next generation leaders in order to further their growth. I've also set myself the task of witnessing about Jesus to non-Christians once a week.

Health care, (exercise, sleep, diet) study aimed at improving my ministry and personal development, receiving mentoring myself, quality time with my children, Bible reading and intercession time, considering the vision of the church—all things that previously I thought were important but I somehow didn't get around to having time for, I've increasingly been able to get to grips with.

If God had not brought me out of a life bound up in manuscript deadlines and reacting to sudden crises—in other words, if I had not escaped from my 'torture situation'—what would have happened to me? I would probably have burned out, or caused problems for my church or my family, or at the very least I would have carried on filling up my life with empty and irrelevant activity.

The absolute necessities

The first step of mentoring is listening. The second step is recognising the work that God is already doing in the other person's life, and celebrating it together. Then the third step is helping the mentee to focus on the essentials. It might seem like there are many important things, but 'only one thing is needed' (Luke 10:42)—the one thing that God tells us that we need to deal with right at this moment. So that the mentee can discover that one thing for themselves, the mentor must help them to grasp their current situation, to see their future, to envisage the process leading to the achievement of their goals, and to recognise the immediate next step. Sometimes an effective way to achieve this is for the mentor to share the concerns that he is grappling with himself.

The marathon trainer Yoshio Koide is known for his relaxed way of training runners. One of the reasons why runners are drawn to his unusual training style is perhaps because he, although well past 60 years old himself, always runs along with them. There is a spirit which can only be conveyed by one fighting the same fight, (Hebrews 4:15-16) because it speaks of the mentor's own self-discipline.

Setting out
the options

It's always the mentee's choice

The wrong solution

In 1990, I emigrated to America. Soon afterwards, the aftershave lotion that I had brought from Japan ran out, so I went out to the local supermarket and bought an American brand of aftershave. It felt very refreshing once I had put it on, and so I came to like that particular brand, putting it on not just after shaving but any time my skin was itchy. When I put it on, the itching quickly went away, and so I was happy that I had found such a good lotion.

But a little while later, my hands, face, and head felt itchy quite often. To begin with, I thought it was because of California's arid climate. I was so busy that I didn't think much about it, but put on more and more of this wonderful lotion. Eventually, it seemed like I was getting itchy all the time, and so I thought that something must be wrong. Then I realised it: the lotion itself was the cause of the problem.

Even though the lotion took away the itchiness for a short time, it was too much stimulation for my skin. As proof, when I stopped using the lotion, my symptoms went away. To put it another way, what I thought was the solution was actually the cause of the problem. There were at least three issues here:

- It seemed like it was giving quick results.

- A habit had been formed.

- I didn't consult anyone about it.

Not alone but together

Once I had got the wrong impression, and my behaviour became a habit, I carried on with a mistaken judgment and mistaken activity based on a mistaken assumption. We humans easily make mistakes. When Jesus compared us to sheep, this was not inappropriate. Apparently sheep have weak eyesight and fixate on the pasture right before their eyes, and so they get lost easily. For them, another person's viewpoint is essential.

In the professional sports world, the greater a player becomes, the more they invest in various types of specialized coaching. Even when Tiger Woods is out playing around the world, he takes videos of his swing and sends them over the Internet for regular check-ups with his coach. Carrying on the theme of golf, as well as having coaches for technical excellence, Woods has advisors on how he should approach the course, coaches to support his physical condition such as health and muscle strength, and coaches to encourage his psychological stability and strength.

Professional sportsmen look for this kind of mentoring because they believe that there is a risk that if you go it alone, you can end up believing that a mistaken idea is the truth; rather, for personal improvement, growth and success, we need the co-operation of others. In the letter to the Colossians, we are encouraged to 'let the word of Christ dwell in you richly, teaching and exhorting one another with all wisdom.' (3:16) For Christians too, it is impossible to grow on one's own. We need to fellowship together and to encourage one another.

Words that draw out abilities

I remember a demonstration made in Florida in 1997 by Timothy Gallwey, who is well known as a mentor to organisations like IBM and Coca-Cola. In a large hall, he invited an older lady, who looked like she might not be very good at catching a ball, onto the stage.

He said, 'Watch the seam of the ball and tell me which way it is spinning. It doesn't matter if you don't catch it.' Then he threw a few balls. Without putting out her hands to catch the first ball, she said 'it's turning from right to left.' Then after the second ball, as well as saying 'turning right' or 'going from down to up', she began quite naturally to catch the balls. As everyone was able to see from their seats, he gradually increased the speed of the balls that he was throwing.

Eventually she was able to catch even very difficult balls with apparent ease. Because through being mentored she had maintained her focus on the ball, she was freed from thinking 'I'd be embarrassed to drop a catch in front of all these people' or 'I'm not a very sporty person.' So by the mentor saying beforehand 'it doesn't matter if you don't catch it,' she was able to get away from the compulsive thought of needing to catch it.

By putting the appropriate option before this woman, Gallwey succeeded in drawing out the ability that she already had. If he had put pressure on her to catch, saying something like 'Look at the ball more!' or 'Bend your knees!', she would have felt disorientated standing on the stage. She would probably have hated catching even more than she did previously.

How to set out the options

The fourth step of mentoring is laying out the options. There are two ways of setting out these options. The first method involves asking good questions to help the mentee become able to see their own situation and problems for themselves. This should lead to them specifying the objectives that they should be aiming for, the process that will lead to the fulfillment of those objectives, and finally the areas that they should focus on from their current position. This way the mentee will be given 'awareness,' like someone distinguishing their own features in a mirror, and be able to choose the path that they should take.

Another option is for the mentor and mentee to appear together before God who is their rightful leader.

I'm sure that many readers, on reading the example about catching the ball, thought about the story of Peter walking on the water. While Peter fixed his eyes only on Jesus, he was able to walk on the water. But, 'when he saw the wind, he was afraid and, began to sink.' (Matthew 14:30) If we 'keep our eyes fixed on Jesus, the pioneer and perfecter of our faith,' (Hebrews 12:2) we can relax, supported by God, and live in a way that exhibits the gifts and abilities that He has given us.

In this place of presence, 'whether you turn to the right or to the left, your ears will hear a voice behind you, saying, "This is the way; walk in it."' (Isaiah 30:21, NIV)

John 10 gives us a picture of a shepherd who calls out his sheep's names and whose sheep listen to his voice. This is opposed to the values of most modern people, who rely too much on analysing information and making decisions rationally. However, if we turn our ears together to what God is saying to the mentee, the mentor and the mentee can both experience the patience and sincerity of Jesus our shepherd.

One thing that coaches who are giving spiritual insight must be aware of is the danger of being too conclusive or forceful. As much as possible, it must be the mentee who makes the choices, and so it is important to leave space for the mentee to refuse that advice, to have reservations, or to choose a different path altogether.

Challenging the will

The prequisite for growth
is the desire to change

When will you start?

In November 2000, Tom Nebel and his team came to
Japan and ran a mentoring seminar in four locations.
Nebel had worked training pioneer evangelists around
the Great Lakes, who had planted churches but found
it difficult for them to grow further. However, as the
workers that he had mentored developed, the success
rate of pioneer evangelism went from 25% to 95%. In
nine years of work, he has now been able to assist in
the planting of 40 churches.

The seminar he did in Osaka was not merely lectures
but the attendees got into groups of three and had the
opportunity to mentor each other. We got into groups
with those sitting near us, and so various mentoring
arrangements were born.

One young man in his teens ended up mentoring a
veteran pastor. Since that young man had been mentored himself, he drew on that experience, listening
kindly to what the pastor had to say, looking for the

good points and celebrating together, and focusing him in on the essentials.

This pastor's problem was that he was so busy, he did not take the time to still himself before God. The young man went through various options with the pastor to try to solve this. Choosing from those options, the pastor decided to have his devotions at six-thirty in the morning just after he got up. Following the four steps of (1) listening, (2) celebrating, (3) focusing and (4) laying out the options, the young man was able to help the pastor to reflect on what God wanted him to do.

However, mentoring does not end there. The young man next asked the pastor, 'when will you start?' The pastor replied that he would start from the next day. Then the young man asked, 'can I ask you about your devotions the next time we meet?' The pastor asked him to call him after a few days.

Finally the young man asked, 'Is there anything I can do to help?' The pastor answered, 'Could you call me at six-thirty every three days or so? Even if you wake my wife up, she'll go straight back to sleep. But at least if I'm thinking that you might call, I'll know that I have to get up!' In the end, the young man did call every few days for a few weeks, and helped the pastor to get into a new habit.

Lifestyle change

The final step of mentoring is challenging the mentee's will. If the mentee knows God's plan for them, experiences the warmth of God's love but does not follow it up with some kind of concrete activity, he is like the 'foolish man who builds his house on the sand.' (Matthew 7:26)

Mentoring should not just stop at satisfying the mentee's intellectual curiosity and emotional needs, but should lead to them making a decision to follow Christ and to accept the will of God in their everyday life.

Wolfgang Simson defines Christianity as follows:

> Christianity is not the general term for the act of attending a series of religious meeting, it is the living way itself. Before they were called Christians, followers of Christ were called "people of the Way". One of the reasons they were called that is because they were people who had found, as the name implies, "the living way".

The essence of the church is not to be understood by attending a series of religious meetings. The church is not an assembly led by a clergyman in a place planned and set aside for experiencing Jesus; the essence of the church should be understood as "a way of living led by God." In other words, the followers of Christ live their everyday lives in the midst of a spiritual family.

The pastor we mentioned before was struggling to change his own lifestyle. Maybe there are some people who believe that a pastor should be able to change his lifestyle fairly easily, but actually a pastor more than anyone else faces the peculiar temptation to hide his real self behind the pulpit and continue to preach entirely 'theoretical' sermons. However, this man humbled himself, accepted the help of someone around his own son's age, and, trusting in God, fought to change his way of living. Only this kind of testimony can give a motive for encouraging others. Doctrine alone is not a threat to the devil; Christians have victory over him through the testimonies of those who heard doctrine but then put it into practice. (Revelation 12:11)

The desire to change

The prerequisite to lifestyle change is the will to change. Jesus himself asked people 'what do you want me to do for you?" or 'do you want to be healed?' I believe that God asks us, 'do you really want to live a life that follows Christ?' Starting from that desire awakened by God, we can take a step forward towards maturity. (Philippians 4:13) One of the roles of the mentor is to be a mirror showing the desire that God has planted in the mentee's heart.

Because of this, setting unreasonable goals does no good and a lot of harm. At worst, the mentee will see through the mentor and get discouraged, losing the will to improve, reinforcing a habit of blaming themselves for their failures. The most important thing is for the mentor and mentee together to confirm what God is saying that they need to do at this time.

Giving a practical challenge

The young man's question 'when will you start?' was successful in guiding the pastor's heart towards a practical activity. The journey of a thousand miles starts with a single step. No matter how superb the vision or how emotional the goal, if the first step is not taken it will remain pie in the sky. Perhaps by declaring 'I'll start tomorrow,' the pastor was able to think 'right, let's make that first step.'

The young man's next question, 'can I ask you about your devotions the next time we meet?', can be thought of as bringing about the following four results:

First, it brings to mind a decision made before God.

Second, it provides an opportunity for confession. If the pastor was unable to do it, through confessing his inability he could take the responsibility for his own actions and start again from scratch.

Third, it forms a series of steps. That is, moving from one managable step to another confirms that it is eventually possible to reach the goal.

Fourth, it provides an opportunity for evaluation. It is something that is not obvious unless it is practiced.

And by saying 'is there anything I can do to help?' the young man surely gave the pastor the feeling that he had a friend who would fight this battle with him.

The great mentor Paul commands us to 'rejoice with those who rejoice, weep with those who weep.' (Romans 12:15) This means giving up a lifestyle filled with seeking to be first and choosing a way of living that seeks to reach the goal together with the other person, even if it means coming in in last place.

Finishing well

Getting a lifelong perspective

Life is full of danger

People today are assaulted with many temptations to sin. According to a survey of 10,000 people, 8% of Internet users are suffering from serious sexual impulses or are demonstrating symptoms of sexual addiction. Christians are no exception.

There was an article in an American newspaper which stated the following: 'One out of three people who attended a Promise Keepers rally in 1996 said they were struggling with temptation to look at pornographic magazines.' This tendency is also prevalent amongst the clergy. 'According to a telephone survey of pastors and their households from a prominent Pentecostal denomination, 25% of respondents said that they suffered from addiction to pornography.'

There are various obstacles which can hinder the Christian from 'finishing well.' One of those is, as we mentioned above, sexual temptation. Others include lust for money, pride, desire for power, problems within the household, as well as stagnation through apathy or lack of faith. Many Christians who once had a joyful testimony end up falling into pits of despondency, burn-out or scandal. What should we do about this?

To be honest, there are not many people who can carry out a fulfilled life right to the end. What should be done to overcome these obstacles and run the race of life right to the end? Dr. Bob Clinton, a well-known figure in the world of leadership theory, has researched the lives of those who continued to live a blessed life right to the end, and has drawn out five common characteristics:

- They have a lifelong perspective.

- They had and enjoyed repeated times of spiritual renewal.

- They received special training for self-cultivation.

- They maintained an attitude of learning.

- They had someone that they could consult during life's problems.

The four territories of mentoring

The person who can see a goal to their life, that is, what they want to see when their life is completed, can live a focussed life. In Paul's farewell sermon at Ephesus, he says the following: 'But I do not consider my life worth anything to myself, so that I may finish my task and the ministry that I received from the Lord Jesus, to testify to the good news of God's grace.' (Acts 20:24)

Furthermore, in 1 Corinthians 9:24, he commands us to 'run in such a way as to get the prize.' (NIV) We might say that one of the secrets to why he was so greatly used by God is that he kept a lifelong perspective.

Before Jesus entered into his public ministry, he spent forty days in the wilderness. After that, he returned to Galilee full of the power of the Spirit. He went into the synagogue and read the Bible, declaring that the Scripture had been fulfilled that day. (Luke 4:22) We can clearly see from this how strong a sense of calling he had and how it affected his life. The person who is aware of what their life is for can live a life that is focussed. Spending time before God receiving His plan for one's life is the key to walking a victorious life. God, the great artist, can use the mentor as a medium to bring the mentee's life to fulfillment in at least the following four areas:

- To impress upon the mentee the importance of having a lifelong perspective.

- To propose taking time for renewal and spiritual refreshment to help attain their life's calling.

- To point out to them the importance of appropriate training and self-cultivation.

- Through the mentor's own attitude of lifelong learning, to be a living witness to the joy of continually seeking after Christ.

Raising up people who can raise up others

This is how the mentor can be one who raises up people, but the number of people that a single mentor can affect during their life is limited. If a coach has a fantastic ministry and develops people who can work in tandem with Christ, but they do not become mentors for others, the chain of development stops at that first generation. The mentee must be raised up so that they can become a mentor to others.

For instance, a coffee maker can make coffee, but it can't make more coffee makers. But living things are part of a cycle where a parent does not merely give birth to a child, but the child then grows up to become a parent and give birth to children. If the mentoring relationship is alive, it must pass on its genes to the next generation.

Previously, we said that a lifelong viewpoint is necessary in order to finish well, but that is not enough if this country is to be discipled. I believe that when leaders come forward who have a vision for raising up people who can raise up others, Japan's churches will be able to hear the voice of God who says 'sing, O barren woman, you who never bore a child.' (Isaiah 54:1)

God's dream

A friend of mine saw a vision. Various kinds of seed were being sown in a field. In the places where the different seeds were planted were sticks with pictures of flowers on the ends. Then, an angel poured water on those places. As my friend watched, he realised that each seed was a person's life, and that God himself was raising up each one and bringing forth a flower that He had marvellously purposed for each individual.

The person who raises us up is none other than God Himself. If we end up thinking 'I will develop that person,' we may need to go through some kind of wilderness experience before we begin ministry again. All that the coach can do is to prepare an environment where the power of the life that God has already given that person can be set free. The wonderful privilege of being a mentor is to be able to catch a glimpse of what God wants to do in someone's life, what He wants to achieve through their life—the dream that God has for them.